Purrrfect SCOTTISH CATS

Purrrrfect

SCOTTISH CATS

Alison Mary Fitt

Illustrations by Bob Dewar

BLACK & WHITE PUBLISHING

First published 2003
by Black & White Publishing Ltd
99 Giles Street, Edinburgh, EH6 6BZ

ISBN 1 902927 95 8

A CIP catalogue record for this book
is available from The British Library.

Design by Creative Link
Printed and bound by BookPrint SL, Barcelona

BLANTYRE.

THE DARK CONTINENT

In a purrrallel Scottish universe,
it's reigning kits and mogs . . .

Whiskers Wallace

A brave cat with single intent,
On fighting for Scotland was bent.
His troops he did rally,
From doorstep and alley,
And 'FURRRDOM!' he yowled as they went.

Robert the Puss

For King Robert the Puss, things looked grave,
As he sat all alone in that cave.
Then he heard someone cry,
'You must try, try and try!' –
Thus a spider saved Scotland the Brave.

Ginger Knox

Ginger Knox, from his pulpit on high,
At his cat congregation did cry,
'You're all sinners indeed,
And you'd better take heed,
Or you'll go straight to Hell when you die!'

Mary, Queen of Cats

Mary went to the scaffold and said,
'Can you chop off my tail, not my head?'
But cruel Lizzie said, 'No!
Your head's got to go —
I'll be far better off when you're dead!'

Fluffy MacDonald

Bravely Fluffy MacDonald did row,
O'er to Skye, wi' Prince Charlie in tow.
Her fur got all soggy,
Poor drookit wee moggy —
But his thanks gave her face such a glow.

Rabbie Burmese

A poet called Rabbie Burmese
Wrote stanzas with consummate ease.
After hoors at the plooghin',
He'd get doon tae some wooin' —
He's weel versed on the birds and the bees.

David Livingstom

Off to Africa's dark continent,
Doctor Livingstom, missionary, went.
And, despite all the dangers,
He brought God to the strangers,
But, alas, his nine lives were soon spent.

Alexander Graham Tinkle-Bell

An inventor whose name is well known,
He concocted the very first phone.
And so, thanks to his skill,
We can blether at will,
On the mewbiles that most of us own.

Charles Rennie Mogintosh

A fine architect named Mogintosh
Designed tea-rooms where fat cats could nosh.
All his chairs cost a mint —
They would leave you quite skint —
Well, it IS Art Mewveau for your dosh.

ART
MEWVEAU
(GAUDÍ)

The Lap Ness Monster

He's a monster who does love to eat —
He has starters, a main course and sweet.
Having tried Atkins' diet,
He prefers to deep-fry it —
Now his weight makes his poor owner greet.

Hairy Lauder

As a mewsic-hall mog with a lilt,
Great rappaw with his fans Hairy built.
The cats joined in the chorus,
Of 'A Wee Deochan Dorus',
And they howled when he waggled his kilt!

John Moggy Baird

Moggy Baird's televisual dream
Had an aerial, dials and a screen.
But those satellite dishes,
They were not in his wishes —
Oh, except if they're filled up with cream.

Jimmiaow Shand

Jimmiaow Shand with his band he did play,
At some mighty grand dos in his day.
But the love o' his life
Were the wee halls in Fife,
Where they birled to a reel or catspey.

Rev I Miaow Jolly

This greetin'-faced cat on the telly
Makes you laugh 'til you get a sore belly.
With his weary 'Hullo-o-o',
And his 'tails' full of woe –
Switch off??? No, not on your nelly!

Deborah Purr

Yowl Brynner cried, 'Help me because
My kits need a firm pair of paws.'
To Deborah's dismay,
They soon romped away.
Siameasy? If only it was.

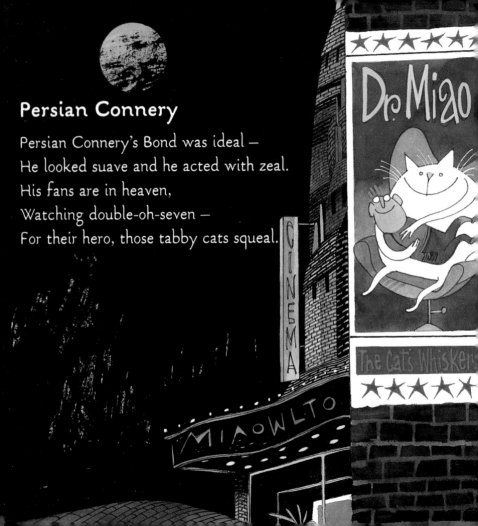

Persian Connery

Persian Connery's Bond was ideal —
He looked suave and he acted with zeal.
His fans are in heaven,
Watching double-oh-seven —
For their hero, those tabby cats squeal.

Denis Claw

And the fans are beginning to roar,
Yes, it's Claw on the ba' – will he score?
Now the net's in his sight –
But the angle is tight –
IT'S A GOAL! CLAWMAN'S DONE IT ONCE MORE!

Siamese Torrance

Such mognificent golf he can play,
In Britain or the U HISS of A.
He slinks and he struts,
As he skilfully putts —
He can face Tiger Woods any day.

David Cooltab

From his sleek new McLaren he smiles,
For he knows it can eat up those miles.
If he sees a cool puss,
He just steps on the juice,
And they're off for a night on the tiles.

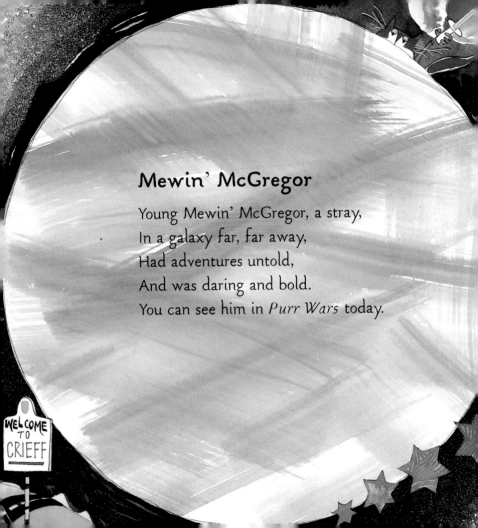

Mewin' McGregor

Young Mewin' McGregor, a stray,
In a galaxy far, far away,
Had adventures untold,
And was daring and bold.
You can see him in *Purr Wars* today.